Preface

The number of people approaching the Imperial War Museum's Department of Printed Books for information about the military service of individuals from earlier generations of their families has risen steadily over the past decade and shows no sign of abating. In 1998, the 80th Anniversary of Armistice Day elicited an even larger than usual November post bag and there was a remarkable degree of interest when we 'went on the road' with a stand at the Family History Fair, London in May 1999.

Some years ago we were able to produce a quick reference guide on tracing individual service records - our original *Information Sheet 15*. Updated and divided into sheets for each of the services, this has proved very popular but it is clear that many 'lay' enquirers also need some further background information.

This, and the need for a further update of our information sheets, has prompted us to devise the *Tracing Your Family History* series.

Led by Mary Wilkinson, a team comprising Sarah Paterson, Allison Duffield and Angela Wootton is largely responsible for the hard work of compiling this new series. Allison Duffield has undertaken the research required for this guide on the Merchant Navy. We have benefited too from the support and advice of staff in the Exhibits and Firearms, Marketing and Museum Services Departments, and in the Research and Information, and Design and Production Offices.

Lastly, we are grateful to other present and former members of staff of the Department of Printed Books, including those in the Public Services section of the Department who answer the lion's share of family history enquiries received by telephone. Although we owe a debt of gratitude to all past staff members who have helped to build up our present expertise and resources, we would particularly like to remember the late Martin Taylor, who would have been delighted by the production of these guides.

Richard Golland
Keeper, Department of Printed Books

About the Museum

One of the founding principles behind the establishment of the Imperial War Museum (IWM) in 1917, was its function as a collective memory. Although the original plan for listing the names of the fallen as an intrinsic part of the building never materialised, the Museum has always regarded the individual and his or her experience as being of paramount importance. In his opening address in June 1920, Sir Alfred Mond 'the father of the Imperial War Museum' declared the hope that the collection would be made *'so complete that every individual, man or woman, sailor, soldier, airman or civilian who contributed, however obscurely, to the final result, may be able to find in these galleries an example or illustration of the sacrifice he made or the work he did, and in the archives some record of it.'* Consequently, today the Museum can offer a wealth of material to the family history researcher.

A walk around the narrative displays on the major conflicts of the century at the main site in Lambeth Road can help provide a context for a relative's service. There are also additional sites at Duxford in Cambridgeshire, HMS *Belfast*, moored next to Tower Bridge on the Thames, and the Cabinet War Rooms in Whitehall, which provide additional illumination on air warfare, naval activities and war politics respectively.

The scope of the Museum encompasses all conflict since 1914 concentrating on British and Commonwealth involvement. In an age of total war, every family in the United Kingdom has been affected in some way. The last decade has seen a marked increase in the study of family history. From schoolchildren interviewing grandparents, to local historians writing com-memorative histories, the burgeoning growth of this popular activity has made it a real industry. Many of the individuals engaged in research can learn much from the material housed at the Imperial War Museum – original art works and objects of war, personal letters and diaries, contemporary film and photographs, retrospective recorded interviews with participants, and the invaluable collection of printed materials, journals, maps and ephemera. Research may be done in any of the seven reference departments of the Museum - the Departments of Art, Documents, Printed Books and Exhibits and Firearms, and the Film and Video, Photograph and Sound Archives. Access to these collections is both welcomed and encouraged, although a prior appointment is usually necessary. Initial approaches can be made by telephone, letter or e-mail, and staff can provide advice about how to proceed with an enquiry and what materials might be available.

For the family researcher, the first port of call will generally be the Department of Printed Books. This constitutes a national reference library containing well over 125,000 books and pamphlets, 15,000 volumes of periodicals and an impressive range of individual maps and ephemeral items, such as ration-books, propaganda leaflets and song-sheets. It is important to stress that the Imperial War Museum does not hold any personal service records or official documentation, although through both this booklet and our normal enquiry service, we can offer advice on what and where remaining sources may still be found. We do have a wide range of items in our collections which will assist the researcher. These can all be consulted under one roof, with experienced staff on hand to direct and help answer enquiries.

The primary aim of the present booklet is to help the enquirer find out about individuals who served in the Merchant Navy. Some basic information is given in the following paragraphs and useful book titles which will help those unfamiliar with the subject, are given in the bibliography at the end. All of these titles are held by the Museum and can be consulted in the reading room, but, for those unable to make a personal visit, full publication details are given to enable alternative copies to be ordered through the public library system wherever possible. Addresses of the various institutions which may assist can also be found conveniently listed in Appendix III. Detailed information about merchant seamen who have been taken prisoner of war will not be found in here, nor will you find advice on sources for the Commonwealth forces. If you do have any queries on either of these subjects please consult us for separate guidance.

Sincere efforts have been made to ensure that the information contained in this booklet is accurate. If any errors have inadvertently been made, we would appreciate it if these could be drawn to our attention so that amendments can appear in later editions.

Organisation of the Merchant Navy

Merchant ships and seamen have always played a vital role in British economic life, not least in wartime. In medieval times there was no such thing as a 'fighting navy,' only merchant ships engaged in trade on behalf of the Monarch. When war broke out the Monarch called upon these merchant ships to come to the country's aid. It was not until the early part of the 18th Century that the 'sea services' were separated into the Merchant Navy and the Royal Navy. When the Royal Navy became established as a fighting force, Parliament ordered all merchant ships to fly a distinctive flag. This flag was to be the Red Ensign, in the canton of which (top corner next to the flagstaff), was placed a small Union Jack. This is the flag which many in merchant service now refer to as the "Old Red Duster."

By 1914 and the mobilisation of the Grand Fleet, heavy demands were made on the Merchant Navy for ships to carry fuel, ammunition and stores, to support the naval forces and to transport the Army to foreign countries. At this time, the administration of the Merchant Navy was divided between the Board of Trade and the Admiralty Transport Department. In 1916 the New Ministries and Secretaries Act set up the Ministry of Shipping to control and regulate merchant shipping for government purposes and to provide and maintain an efficient supply of shipping in support of the war effort. In 1917 the Admiralty Transport Department was transferred to the Ministry of Shipping, as was the control of shipbuilding, formerly shared between the Admiralty and the Board of Trade. This new Ministry of Shipping was dissolved in March

1921 and its responsibilities passed to the Mercantile Marine Department of the Board of Trade.

Up until 1922, the Merchant Navy had been variously referred to as the *Mercantile Marine*, the *Merchant Service* or the *Merchant Marine*, but by Royal decree was now to be officially known as the Merchant Navy. This 'honour' was served on the Merchant Service in gratitude for their services during the First World War. During the 1920s and 1930s the Merchant Navy returned to its primary functions of maritime trading and transport.

In October 1939 the Ministry of Shipping was re-established to undertake the functions of the Sea Transport Division, the Mercantile Marine Department of the Board of Trade. Control of shipbuilding was transferred to the Admiralty in February 1940. However, the Ministry of Shipping and Ministry of Transport merged in May 1941 to form the Ministry of War Transport. This Ministry was divided into the Ship Management Division, Sea Transport Division and the Marine Crews Division. In 1946 the word 'War' was dropped from the title.

After the Second World War the Ministry of Transport, with its various departments and in conjunction with the shipping companies and seamen's unions, continued to be responsible for the functions of the Merchant Navy. However, the second half of the 20th Century saw a great reduction in the Merchant Navy Fleet, although they were still called upon for support in times of crisis. For example, several of the remaining tankers, liners and even tugs and trawlers, were requisitioned by the Ministry of Defence for service in the Falklands Conflict of 1982. Fewer were available for service during the Gulf War of 1991.

SEAMEN

When the Merchant Shipping Act of 1854 was passed, conditions for seamen were much improved as the Act regulated the method of engagement (joining) and discharge (leaving). Shipping offices were set up in the principal ports, Articles of Agreement were drawn up between the owners of the vessels and the crews, and official logs were started. New shipping companies appeared which resulted in further improvements in the welfare and conditions of seamen - mainly as a result of 'competition.'

In peacetime, the crew of a merchant ship is 'Signed-on-Articles' before a Shipping Master at the port from which the ship is sailing. The Articles, or *T 124* as the document is officially known, are read out to all intending to 'sign on.' Every member of the crew signs their name to the Agreement. Rates of pay and occupation are recorded against the name.

It is difficult to lay down hard and fast rules about the number of officers and crew carried by a ship as their duties will vary according to the size and class of the vessel, and the type of trade or transport in which she is involved. Under Board of Trade regulations a minimum number was laid down, but all too often this minimum was strictly adhered to resulting in a worsening of conditions for the seamen. This problem was soon addressed by the rise of seamen's unions.

OFFICERS

Merchant Navy officers command by their example and character alone, as they have no Naval Discipline Act to back them up when enforcing orders, especially as in most cases the crew have not had the training or discipline given to Royal Navy personnel. Strictly speaking there are no officers in the Merchant Navy, only *Masters* and *Mates*. Therefore, the following officer titles are, in the main, honorary.

A *Commodore* is the title given to the most senior Master in the shipping company. He will be in command of what is usually the largest and newest vessel in the fleet, designated the 'flagship,' as the shipping company's house flag may be flown. Next in line is the *Captain*, more commonly referred to as the *Master*. In the case of smaller vessels the term used is *Skipper*. The Master is responsible for the safe navigation of the vessel and the efficiency of the officers and crew under his command. He is also responsible for any passengers carried on board. The *Chief Officer*, or *First Mate*, is the 'second-in-command.' He is responsible for the smooth running and navigation of the vessel and is in charge of the on-deck personnel. He is also responsible for any cargo carried. However, he does not stand watches, which is normally undertaken by the *Second, Third* or *Fourth Officers* (or *Mates*). In addition, many larger vessels carry junior officers as *Cadets, Midshipmen* or *Apprentices*, as part of their on-board training.

Below-deck the *Chief Engineer* is responsible for all the Engine-Room Staff and reports directly to the Master. Next in line is the *Assistant Chief Engineer*, followed by the *Second, Third* and *Fourth Engineers* all of whom take part in engine-room watches. Depending on the size of the vessel and the number of passengers carried, *Surgeons*, or *Medical Officers*, are also carried on board. Originally, the *Wireless Officer* was not strictly speaking a member of the Merchant Navy but an employee of the radio company lent to the shipping company. This was to change in times of war, as were the positions of *Signal Officers*.

CREW

The *Boatswain* is the 'buffer' between the officers and the men and is the most senior rating in charge of the crew in the upper-deck. The *Carpenter* also has his own staff and is responsible for any repairs to the vessel's equipment, including the all important steering-gear. The *Quartermasters* are those who have had a great deal of experience at sea, their duties are numerous and include taking a turn at the wheel. They are chosen from the group of *Able-Bodied Seamen* (or *Leading Seamen*). Next are the *Ordinary Seamen* and *Boys*, who are seamen in training.

Below-deck is the Engine-Room Staff, made up of specialists according to the size and type of the vessel and its cargo. The *Donkeyman* is the most senior engine-room rating. In addition, larger vessels may carry *Greasers*, who are experienced Firemen, to assist the Engineers in the smooth running of the machinery and be responsible for the work of the other Firemen and Trimmers. In coal-fuelled vessels the *Firemen* had to keep the fires burning beneath the boilers and the *Trimmers* were responsible for the supply of coal from the bunkers to the stockhold. However, in oil-fuelled vessels there was little need for a large staff.

In large passenger ships the *Purser's* Department is of great importance, as it is responsible for the victualling of the ship and the comfort of the passengers. The Purser would be assisted by the *Chief Steward*, who in turn would be assisted by the *Deputy* (or *Assistant*) *Stewards*. The Steward's Department is made up of *Cooks*, *Butchers* and *Bakers* in the galleys and *Waiters* for duties in the dining-rooms, cabins and decks.

However, since the 'manning' of a merchant vessel was dependent on the size and type of the vessel, in times of war the complement and their duties changed radically as many merchant vessels were requisitioned and converted for war work. In the case of larger vessels, a regular naval Captain was appointed to command the vessel. The original Captain/Master, if not already in the Royal Navy Reserves, was given a temporary commission as a Commander and retained to advise the naval Captain. Gunnery officers, Signal officers and a number of naval ratings were also appointed for general duties. Nearly all the ship's engineers were normally retained as they were used to the workings of their vessel's engines. Merchant Navy officers were often given temporary commissions, equal to their 'rank' in peacetime. In many cases the crew were already in the Royal Fleet Reserve or Royal Naval Reserve and so adapted well to the change. However, few were signals experts, so men from the Royal Naval Volunteer Reserve took over these duties.

Smaller vessels, like coastal craft and trawlers, were also requisitioned for a vast range of wartime duties. Generally, the complement remained the same, with the addition of naval Petty Officers for signals duties. The Skipper was given a warrant rank in the Royal Naval Reserve. Some of the crew were already in the Reserves so would have had some training in the use of gunnery. After the periods of war had ended merchant seamen returned to their more 'normal' duties.

SHIPPING

The number of merchant ship types has grown considerably over the years, mainly due to the increased demands made by world trade and transportation. These vessels fall into four main groupings: *Passenger vessels* which include holiday and excursion vessels, as well as pleasure craft; *Cargo vessels*, which, as the name suggests, transports all types of cargo as well as, on occasion, a few passengers; *Fishing vessels*; and finally *Auxiliary* and *Support vessels*. Although too numerous to mention individually, the main types of vessel in service during the 20th Century are described below.

The 'first' among the passenger vessels, because of their size and prestige, are the *passenger liners*, which are seen by many as floating palaces. These liners have a very large passenger capacity and a fairly large cargo space. Although smaller than the liner, the *cross-channel vessels* are used for much shorter voyages between the United Kingdom and Europe. These include 'short-hop' *ferries*, transporting passengers on a daily basis. However, they are sometimes regarded as 'holiday' vessels like the *paddle-steamer*. Although these steamers once sailed the oceans, they are now used for holiday traffic and special excursions in and around our coastlines. They still offer a high standard of comfort for passengers. Finally, another passenger carrying vessel is the *yacht*. Although mainly used for cruising and sailing many were built specifically for the purpose of racing.

The *cargo liner* is similar in size and speed to the passenger liner, but concentrates on the carriage of special cargoes rather than passengers. However, many have the facilities to carry a few passengers. Again, they sail all over the world but run to a tight schedule, usually between two ports only. Much of their special cargo is foodstuffs; meat, dairy produce and fruit, depending on the size of the carrier. 'Bulk' cargo is usually loose grain, sugar etc. Another type of cargo carrier is the *tramp*, often referred to as the *universal carrier*. They carry a large variety of cargoes and can be chartered for work in any part of the world, often for long periods. Since they were not involved in 'regular' trade the tramp was seen as a much cheaper alternative to the cargo liner. Other 'specialist' cargo carriers include *ore carriers* and *oil tankers*. Both are similar in size, but the latter is usually referred to as the most important class of cargo carrier in existence during the 20th Century. There are two classes of tanker, the clean tanker which carries petrol, paraffin etc. and the dirty tanker carrying heavy fuel oils and lubricants. These tankers also transport their cargoes world-wide. Closer to home we find the *coasters* and *colliers*, which as their names suggest, carry freight and coal around our coastlines and in some cases to localised ports in Europe.

Trawlers and *drifters* differ from cargo vessels in that they leave their home ports with no cargo and return with a cargo of fish. Some of the larger trawlers are really ocean-going vessels, with the smaller craft intended for around our coastlines. The drifters are smaller vessels, often of wooden construction. They rarely venture far from their home port. The difference between a trawler and a drifter is that the trawler trawls (or tows) when fishing, towing a large conical shaped net behind her. The drifter literally drifts when fishing, putting out a vertical wall of net in front of her.

The auxiliary and support vessels, similar in size to the fishing vessels, are the *tugs*. Large ocean-going tugs are often involved in salvage operations and have to be powerful in speed and towing in order to bring a vessel in for repair. Often referred to as *rescue tugs*, they must not be confused with *rescue ships*, as the latter is concerned with the saving and accommodation of personnel, whereas the tug is interested only in the salvage of the 'distressed' vessel for repair. If repairs are not possible, then *salvage ships* will be called in for purely salvage purposes. Smaller tugs are used for ship-handling, for example, when they are docking. They are also used in the handling of river barges. Unless the entrances to ports and harbours are kept clear of sand, rock or mud, ships would not be able to enter. This is the work of the *dredger*. One type of dredger is the *bucket dredger*, which uses its buckets to clear the blockages. The material is then discharged into the hull of the dredger itself or into little ships operating on either side of the dredger, called *hoppers*. Other types are the *sand sucker* and the *grab dredger*. *Cable-layers* operate both in mid-ocean and off our coastlines. As the name suggests, they are concerned with the laying, raising and repairing of cables.

In the past, merchant vessels could easily be transformed into warships when the need arose as most were already armed and able to look after themselves. However, during the 20th Century merchant vessels had not been fundamentally designed for weaponry. Therefore in times of war, when they were requisitioned, they had to undergo a variety of conversions in order to accommodate the addition of gun mountings.

Although still involved in the transportation of cargo and passengers, the duties of the merchant fleet changed radically during the First World War. Large liners were converted to *troop carriers* and *hospital ships*. Smaller vessels were fitted out as *armed merchant cruisers*, employed in patrolling the trade routes, enforcing blockades and anti-raider duties. These were probably some of the most important duties as trade routes had to be protected at all times to ensure the safe arrival of foodstuffs, equipment and supplies. Paddle-steamers became *minesweepers* and *troop carriers* and some cross-channel vessels were converted to *seaplane carriers*. Some cargo vessels were employed as *Q-ships*. These were heavily armed, but disguised as 'normal' cargo carriers in order to decoy enemy submarines to the surface before engaging them at close range. Trawlers and drifters were employed in a variety of duties. The larger vessels were used for patrol work and the smaller ones for minesweeping. Other vessels were used as *base, depot* and *repair ships*.

Vessels of the merchant fleet were again requisitioned during the Second World War for duties similar to those described above. However, the main difference between the two World Wars was the growth and efficiency of air power. This led to a programme of anti-aircraft conversions. Many merchant vessels were used for *anti-aircraft escorts* for convoys and for coastal work. The latter duties were normally carried out by converted paddle-steamers.

Another new range of vessels came into being during the Second World War. These included *infantry assault ships* and *landing craft*. Most were purpose built, but many of the infantry assault ships were former passenger and cargo liners, which had originally served as armed merchant cruisers. Other merchant conversions included *headquarters ships, fighter direction ships, landing craft carriers, ocean* and *armed boarding vessels, maintenance vessels* and *amenities ships*.

The post Second World War era saw a sharp rise in techno-logical changes, leading to the appearance of precision-guided weapons. It was deemed no longer feasible to convert and equip all the aforementioned types of merchant vessels. Hence, the types of merchant vessel conversions were reduced to *troopships, tankers* and *support* and *supply ships* although the Falklands Conflict of 1982 saw three merchant vessels fitted out as *auxiliary aircraft carriers* in support of the helicopter and Sea Harrier operations. The Falklands Conflict also showed that such vessels still needed to be fitted with 'defensive' and 'offensive' armament. Thanks to past experiences and to modern day technology, experimentation and invention, merchant ships are now more 'appropriately' armed in times of crisis.

Service Records

Records of the Merchant Navy can be categorised broadly into two main groups, namely shipping and seamen, neither of which is totally independent of the other. Hence, useful information on seamen is more often than not gleaned from Merchant Navy shipping records. These two groups of records are further divided into the following:

Registers of Seamen's Service
Crew Lists and Agreements
Certificates of Competency and Service
Registration of Shipping
Ships' Log Books

For a more detailed description of these categories please refer to Appendix I.

Detailed below are a number of archives which may be of assistance. Please note that some will only release information to the individual concerned, the surviving next-of-kin or legal beneficiary. In most cases search fees will be levied. In all cases the enquirers are recommended to put their requests in writing, quoting in full, the name and as much factual information as is already known on the service of the individual concerned. If no details are known, some basic information may be available from the *Absent Voters Lists* of 1918 and the *Service Voters Registers* of 1945. These should be held by the relevant local library, town hall or county record office.

Another potential source is the **Family Records Centre, 1 Myddelton Street, London EC1R 1UW** which provides research facilities previously provided at St Catherine's House.

Their records include indexes of births, deaths and marriages since 1837, legal adoptions since 1927 and births, deaths and marriages of some British citizens abroad since the late 18th Century.

Most of the relevant records relating to maritime genealogical research are still held by the **Registry of Shipping and Seamen, Anchor House, Cheviot Close, Parc-ty-Glas, Llanishen, Cardiff CF4 5JA**. Genealogical enquiries to the Registry of Shipping and Seamen must be made in writing, but do not receive priority. Instead primary concern is given to official enquiries concerning welfare, employment, pensions and other legal matters. The initial search fee (if levied) is currently £11.00 with further charges made for any copies supplied.

Personnel records which are no longer restricted are held by the **Public Record Office, Ruskin Avenue, Kew, Richmond, Surrey TW9 4DU**, where they are available to the general public. Please note that the Public Record Office does not generally undertake research on behalf of the public. It is usually necessary to visit in person, taking with you some documentary means of identification in order to obtain a reader's ticket. If a visit is not possible, the Public Record Office will provide a list of 'approved' professional researchers. However, for anyone intending to do their own genealogical research, the Public Record Office has produced invaluable guides to their holdings in the form of published handbooks and a series of records information sheets and leaflets, which can be accessed directly on the PRO website (see Appendix III for details). Of particular note are *Tracing Your Ancestors in the Public Record Office*, 5th edition, edited by Amanda Bevan, and *Records of Merchant Shipping and Seamen* by Kelvin Smith, Christopher T Watts and Michael J Watts.

In addition, there are many records relating to genealogical research available for public consultation at the **Guildhall Library, Lloyd's Marine Collection, Aldermanbury, London EC2P 2EJ** and the **National Maritime Museum, Romney Road, Greenwich, London SE10 9NF**. These institutions hold both primary and secondary sources, some of which are detailed within this text. However, appointments to view their collections must be made in advance of arrival.

REGISTERS OF SEAMEN'S SERVICE

In general, Registers of Seamen, for the period 1913-1940 are to be found at the **Public Record Office** in the Board of Trade files *BT 348*, *BT 349* and *BT 350*. Earlier Registers, and those from 1941, are still held by the **Registry of Shipping and Seamen**.

CREW LISTS AND AGREEMENTS

The Registry of Shipping and Seamen also holds all Crew Lists and Agreements for the period 1939-1950, whereas the **Public Record Office** only holds about 10% of all the remaining Crew Lists and Agreements, up to 1980. These are to be found in the Board of Trade files *BT 99* and *BT 100*. The remaining 90% are held by the **Maritime History Archive, Memorial University of Newfoundland, St John's, Newfoundland A1C 5S7 Canada**. Guides to their holdings are to be found at the Public Record Office. The **National Maritime Museum** holds only a sample.

PASSENGER LISTS

Ships' passenger lists were deposited with the Board of Trade by the various shipping lines although copies, often retained by the line, may be found within the company archives. The lists for the period 1878-1960 are to be found in the **Public Record Office** Board of Trade files *BT 26* for arrivals in United Kingdom ports and *BT 27* for departures from United Kingdom ports. These files are arranged by the port and date of the arrival/departure. There is no index. However, if the name of the vessel is known, the researcher can refer to the Registers of Passenger Lists, 1906-1951 in *BT 32*. No passenger lists are held by the Registry of Shipping and Seamen, the National Maritime Museum or the Guildhall Library.

CERTIFICATES OF COMPETENCY AND SERVICE

Certificates of Competency and Service were issued to Merchant Navy Masters, Mates, Engineers and Cooks on completion of examinations, or by exemption due to long service. These Certificates were recorded in Registers, divided by the type of trade.

The **Public Record Office** holds the Registers of Certificates for Masters and Mates for Foreign Trade, 1881-1921 in the Board of Trade files *BT 123* and for Home Trade, 1854-1921 in *BT 125*. There is a consolidated index to these in *BT 127*. However, since the system of recording the issuing of Certificates changed in 1913, the researcher may also find the files in *BT 317* and *BT 318* of interest. The former records the Master and Mates Certificates Passings and Renewals, 1917-1968, and the latter, the Returns of Passes and Failures of

Examinations for Certificates, 1913-1935. An index to these is soon to become available in *BT 352*.

The **National Maritime Museum** holds many of the successful Applications for Certificates outlined above.

The **Public Record Office** also holds microfilmed copies of the Lloyd's Captains' Registers for the period 1851-1947. These were compiled from the record of Certificates of Competency and Service issued to Masters and can be found in the files *BT 122* and *BT 127*. The originals of the Lloyd's Captains' Registers are still lodged with the **Guildhall Library**.

Certificates of Competency and Service issued to Engineers are also to be found at the **Public Record Office** in *BT 140* (Certificates of Competency, 1870-1921), and in *BT 142* (Certificates of Service, 1862-1921). An index to these registers is contained in *BT 141*. As stated previously, 1913 saw a change in the recording of the issuing of Certificates, therefore records of Engineers' Certificates Passings and Renewals, 1919-1929 are to be found in *BT 320* and Returns of Passes and Failures of Examinations for Engineer Certificates, 1913-1935 in *BT 318*. See also the index in *BT 352*.

The registration of Cooks began in 1908. Registers of Cooks' Certificates of Competency and Service, 1915-1958 are held by the **National Maritime Museum**.

REGISTRATION OF SHIPPING

Records relating to the Registration of Shipping may also assist researchers in that they provide invaluable background information on the vessel, including names of each vessel's

Master and changes in ownership. In 1890 a system of keeping all the papers relating to a vessel, regardless of date, was introduced. They were filed together under the date of the vessel's de-registration.

The records for the period 1891-1955 are to be found at the **Public Record Office** in the Board of Trade files *BT 110* (Transcripts and Transactions). They are filed first by the decade of de-registration, then alphabetically by the name of the vessel. Dates of de-registration are to be found by consulting the *Lloyd's Register of Shipping, Lloyd's Register of Yachts* and the *Mercantile Navy List.*

Lloyd's Register of Shipping is an annual alphabetical list of vessels giving current details on the name, official number, date and place of building, technical description, name of builder, owner, master (up to 1921) and port of registry. Name changes and postings of casualties (up to 1955) are included. Between 1890 and 1947 steamers, motor vessels and sailing vessels were listed separately. An additional section for trawlers and other fishing vessels under 300 tons was introduced in 1922. Please note that the 'annual' period is from July to June.

Lloyd's Register of Yachts was introduced in 1877 and is complementary to the *Lloyd's Register of Shipping* and is similarly arranged. However, no issues were produced for the period 1940-1946 and the publication ceased in 1980.

The Mercantile Navy List was the official list of British registered Merchant vessels. It first appeared in 1850 but ceased publication in 1976. These volumes were arranged similarly to the *Lloyd's Registers*, split into two sections for steamers and sailing vessels; a third section for motor vessels was added in 1922.

The **Public Record Office**, **Registry of Shipping and Seamen**, **Guildhall Library** and **National Maritime Museum** all hold sets of these publications. Unfortunately, the Department of Printed Books holds only a small selection of the *Lloyd's Registers* for the period 1914-1940 and the *Mercantile Navy List* for the period 1913-1966.

LOG BOOKS

Log Books are the records of the life of the vessel and include information on various events which occur during each voyage. Log Books for the period 1914-1918 are held by the **Public Record Office** in the Board of Trade files *BT 165*. The **Registry of Shipping and Seamen** holds those for the period 1939-1950. The Public Record Office also holds only about 10% of the Log Books (with the Crew Lists and Agreements), for the periods 1919-1938 and 1951-1976; the remainder being lodged with the **Maritime History Archive**.

Please note that these Log Books are filed in order of the vessel's official number, which are to be found in the afore-mentioned *Lloyds' Registers* and *Mercantile Navy Lists*. Log Books for the vessels requisitioned by the Admiralty are filed by name in the Admiralty files *ADM 53*.

FISHERMEN AND FISHING VESSELS

From 1884 Crew Lists and Agreements were filed separately. The **Public Record Office** holds about 10% of the records, for the periods up to 1938 and after 1951. These are to be found in the Board of Trade files *BT 144* (up to 1929) and in *BT 99* (after 1929). The remaining records are held by the **Maritime**

History Archive. The **Registry of Shipping and Seamen** holds those for the period 1939-1950.

The certificating of Skippers and Mates began in 1884. The **Public Record Office** holds the Registers containing these Certificates of Competency in *BT 129* and the Registers containing Certificates of Service in *BT 130*. An index is to be found in *BT 138*. However, in 1910 a combined index to Certificates of Competence for Masters, Mates, Engineers and Fishing Officers for Foreign and Home Trade was introduced. This is to be found in the files *BT 352* as detailed previously.

From 1894 all fishing vessels had to be registered. As previously described, relevant records are to be found at the **Public Record Office** in the Board of Trade files *BT 110*. Reference should also be made to the annual volumes of *Lloyd's Register of Shipping* and the *Mercantile Navy List*.

Log Books are also split between the **Public Record Office**, the **Registry of Shipping and Seamen** and the **Maritime History Archive**. However, please note that although Log Books for merchant vessels requisitioned during the First and Second World Wars are to be found in the Admiralty files *ADM 53*, few Logs have survived after 1939 for vessels smaller than an armed merchant cruiser.

ROYAL NAVAL RESERVE

In 1859 provision had been made for the Admiralty to maintain a Reserve recruited from Merchant Seamen and fishermen, who could be called upon for service with the Royal Navy in time of emergency. These men made up the **Royal Naval Reserve**, but the 20th Century saw this Reserve further divided into the Royal Naval Reserve Trawler Section, Royal Naval Volunteer Reserve, Royal Fleet Auxiliaries and Royal Naval Division. For more detailed information on the organisation of the Royal Naval Reserve please refer to *Tracing Your Family History: Royal Navy.*

Officer records for those in service for the period 1908-1950 are held by the **Ministry of Defence, DR(2)A Navy, Bourne Avenue, Hayes, Middlesex UB3 1RF**. Records for those in service after 1950 are held by the **Ministry of Defence, NPP(Acs)1E Centurion Building, Grange Road, Gosport, Hampshire PO13 9XA**. The records held by the Ministry of Defence are not open to the public, so enquiries must be made in writing. The search fee (if levied) is currently £25.00.

The only records currently available for public consultation are those for the period 1862-1907 in the Admiralty files *ADM 240* at the **Public Record Office**. Records from 1908 up to 1920 will, hopefully, be available from Summer 2000.

An officer's career in the Royal Naval Reserves can also be traced through the editions of the *Navy List*, published continually from 1814. These contain seniority lists, cross-referred to individual ships, which in turn list their complement of officers. During the First and Second World Wars much of the usual information was omitted from the published editions of the *Navy List* and confined to confidential editions for 'service use' only. A full set is held by the **Public Record Office** and the **National Maritime Museum**, but the Department of Printed Books holds a near complete run, including many of the confidential editions, for the period 1914 to date.

Generally, records for Merchant seamen who joined the Royal Naval Reserve are still held by the **Registry of Shipping and Seamen**, although the **Public Record Office** holds a selection of 'ratings' records for the period 1913-1941 in the Board of Trade files *BT 164*, with a smaller selection, for the same period, in files *BT 348, BT 349* and *BT 350*.

Medal Records and Awards

Awards for service and acts of gallantry were first made to Merchant seamen in the middle of the 19th Century. This system was administered by the Marine Department of the Board of Trade. Records of awards, made during the 20th Century, are now held by the **Registry of Shipping and Seamen**, **Anchor House**, **Cheviot Close**, **Parc-ty-Glas, Llanishen**, **Cardiff CF4 5JA** although many have been, or are in the process of being, transferred to the Public Record Office.

Records available for public consultation are held by the **Public Record Office**, **Ruskin Avenue**, **Kew**, **Richmond, Surrey TW9 4DU** and the **Guildhall Library**, **Lloyd's Marine Collection**, **Aldermanbury**, **London EC2P 2EJ**.

Campaign medals were awarded for participation in a particular campaign, or for service in time of war. Often a 'clasp' was added to the ribbon of these medals to denote a particular campaign. The 'clasp' was also used to denote second or subsequent awards of Long Service and Good Conduct medals.

These medals can be a useful source for researchers as, during the First World War, they usually included the name and unit details of the recipient, engraved either on the rim, or on the back of the medal. Unfortunately, during the Second World War these medals were not stamped with these details, although arrangements could be made to have this done privately.

For more detailed information on the medals themselves and the range of the awards available, please refer to the publications listed in Appendix IV. Those with internet access may also be interested in the Imperial War Museum's **Website:**

http://www.iwm.org.uk/ex-medal.htm which currently gives information on a limited range of medals, but is regularly updated.

Records of campaign medals, awarded during the First World War, including the 1914-15 Star, British War Medal and Victory Medal, are to be found at the **Public Record Office** in the Admiralty files *ADM 171*, for which there are index volumes available. There is a separate group of files for each medal. Records of the Mercantile Marine Medal are in the process of being transferred to the **Public Record Office**.

Records relating to the award of campaign medals during the Second World War and beyond are still held by the **Registry of Shipping and Seamen**. These medals include the 1939-45 Star, the Africa Star, Atlantic Star, Burma Star, France and Germany Star, Italy Star, Pacific Star and the War Medal.

Gallantry medals were awarded for a particular gallant act. The addition of a 'bar' to the medal ribbon of the original medal, denotes a second or subsequent award for gallant or distinguished service.

The amount of information available on these awards does vary considerably. Notification of an award would normally be published in the *London Gazette*, sometimes accompanied by the citation, being a short description of why the award was made. However, there was often a considerable delay between the date of the award and the date that the notification and citation were published. It should also be noted that, although individuals may have been recommended for a particular medal, another award may have been substituted. Awards notified in either of the two half-yearly honours lists ('New Year' and 'Birthday') are not normally accompanied by a citation.

For the range of the awards available to personnel of the Merchant Navy please refer to the list of abbreviations in Appendix II. For information on the awards themselves, refer to the publications listed in Appendix IV and the Imperial War Museum's Website.

In general, gallantry at sea awards for the period 1856-1981 are to be found at the **Public Record Office** in the Board of Trade files *BT 261* and the Ministry of Transport files *MT 9* (which include the Albert Medals for saving life at sea for the period 1903-1950). However, records of the Lloyd's Medals for Gallantry at Sea are to be found at the **Guildhall Library**. Although these records include some citations, those not available may be obtained from the **Manager's Secretarial Department, Lloyd's, Lime Street, London EC3M 7HL**.

In addition, many Merchant Navy seamen received naval gallantry awards during the First and Second World Wars. Records of these are to be found at the **Public Record Office** in Admiralty files *ADM 116* for the First World War and *ADM 1* for the Second World War. Index volumes are held in *ADM 12*.

The medal offices at the **Registry of Shipping and Seamen** also deal with medal claims and/or replacements. Please note that replacement medals may only be issued to the recipient, or if deceased, to the next-of-kin. It will also be necessary to provide official documentary proof of entitlement.

As stated previously, another good source of reference for medal awards and medal citations is the *London Gazette*. However, at the beginning of the Second World War, the publication of all citations for gallantry awards was suspended. All enquiries regarding citations for gallantry awards not published in the *London Gazette* should be referred to the

Ministry of Defence, Honours and Awards, Room 115 Victory Building, HM Naval Base, Portsmouth, Hampshire PO1 3LS.

The Department of Printed Books holds a near complete run of the *London Gazette* from 1914 but, unfortunately, without a complete set of the all important indexes. However, the **Public Record Office** does hold a full set and researchers may also find copies in some of the larger reference libraries in their area.

Generally the Department of Printed Books holds published sources only, some of which are listed in Appendix IV, but we recommend in particular the volumes of *Seedie's Rolls of Honour and Awards* published by Ripley Registers.

Casualty Records

Casualty records are held by the **Registry of Shipping and Seamen, Anchor House, Cheviot Close, Parc-ty-Glas, Llanishen, Cardiff CF4 5JA**. Those available for public consultation (up to 1972) are at the **Public Record Office, Ruskin Avenue, Kew, Richmond, Surrey TW9 4DU**. Similar records are also held by the **Guildhall Library, Lloyd's Marine Collection, Aldermanbury, London EC2P 2EJ** and the **National Maritime Museum, Romney Road, Greenwich, London SE10 9NF**.

Registers of Births, Deaths and Marriages of passengers at sea were compiled using the ships' Logs. Ships' Mates were also required, by the Registration of Births and Deaths Act of 1874, to report all births and deaths on board ship to the Registrar General of Shipping and Seamen who then reported them, periodically, to the Registrars General of Births, Deaths and Marriages of England and Wales, Scotland or Ireland as appropriate.

Up until 1889 separate series of Registers were kept for seamen and passengers, but in 1890 a combined series was introduced. The various Registers concerning deaths at sea contain name, rank/occupation, age, date of birth, address, date of death, place of death (often in longitude and latitude), cause of death and name, official number and port of registry of the vessel.

To access a death at sea (if an approximate date of death is known) first examine the index books for the year the death was registered. They are organised by the name of the vessel and of the deceased. Then search in the Death Register for the particular year, under the relevant month. Please note that some deaths are registered much later than the date they actually occurred.

The **Public Record Office** holds copies of the Registers and Index volumes of Births, Marriages and Deaths of Passengers and Seamen at Sea, 1891-1972 in the Board of Trade files *BT 334*. Later Registers are kept by the **Registry of Shipping and Seamen**.

When a death at sea occurs on a British vessel, the Master is required to complete a Return of Death. These Returns include name, official number and port of registry of the vessel, date and place of death, name, age, rank/occupation, address and cause of death. The reverse of the form includes an extract of the vessel's Log Book which gives an account of the events which led to the death at sea. However, these accounts were not always included. Returns of Death form the basis of the Death Registers described above.

Surviving Returns of Death, for the periods 1914-1919 and 1939-1964 are held by the **National Maritime Museum**. Few Returns have survived for the period 1920-1938. The **Registry of Shipping and Seamen** holds those from 1965 to date.

When a vessel was lost at sea the Log Book would have been lost with the vessel, therefore the owners of the vessel would submit a copy of the crew list to the Registrar General of Shipping and Seamen. These lists would be used for the registration of the deaths of the crew members. Casualties and Deaths Lists are organised by official number of the vessel. These numbers can be located by consulting the annual volumes of the *Lloyd's Register* and the *Mercantile Navy List*. Death Lists, including those from fishing vessels, for the period 1920-1938 are to be found at the **National Maritime Museum**. Lists for the period 1939-1950 are still held by the **Registry of Shipping and Seamen**.

Records of shipping lost at sea are also available for public consultation at the **Public Record Office**, the **Guildhall Library** and the **National Maritime Museum**.

In addition to the Board of Trade files *BT 110*, at the **Public Record Office**, the researcher should also consult the Ministry of Shipping files *MT 25* as they contain returns and lists of vessels sunk during the First World War, papers on the movement of troops, manning of the Merchant Service, casualties and registration. Records relating to the loss of trawlers for the same period are to be found in the Admiralty files *ADM 137*. For losses during the Second World War see the Ministry of War Transport files *MT 9, MT 15* and *MT 59*. In addition, the Admiralty files *ADM 199* contain much material on the loss of individual vessels, including interviews with survivors.

The **Guildhall Library** holds many excellent sources for information on shipping losses. These include *Missing Vessels Books* for the period 1873-1954, which list those vessels posted 'missing' but whose fate is not known, and the *Lloyd's Loss and Casualty Books*, for the period 1837-1998. Each set of books is accompanied by an index.

The National Maritime Museum holds similar records, including a Shipwreck Index, organised by the date of the loss and by the name of the vessel lost.

Reference should also be made to local records and newspapers as they often contain listings and details of casualties from their areas.

COMMONWEALTH WAR GRAVES COMMISSION

The **Commonwealth War Graves Commission, 2 Marlow Road, Maidenhead, Berkshire SL6 7DX** holds details of the burial place or commemoration site for all those who died in service during the periods 1914-1921 and 1939-1947.

This organisation was established in May 1917 as the **Imperial War Graves Commission**, but changed its name to the **Commonwealth War Graves Commission** in 1960. The Commission decided that all service personnel would be treated equally, being buried close to where they died and with uniform headstones. These graves would be cared for in perpetuity. Individuals with no known grave would have their names carved on a memorial.

As well as having information on the burial site or place of commemoration, the Commission has details of date of death and the unit to which the individual was attached. Often, details of their home address and next-of-kin were included.

Details of those employed in the Merchant Service who were 'buried at sea' during the First and Second World Wars, are recorded in the memorial registers relating to Tower Hill and Liverpool.

It is not possible to visit the Commonwealth War Graves Commission in person, although copies of cemetery and memorial registers can be purchased from them. The Commission may charge a search fee for postal enquiries, but since information is now computerised, it can be accessed freely via their *Debt of Honour* database, **website: http://www.cwgc.org**. Copies of all the Commission's published registers are conveniently located in the Department of Printed

Books' Reading Room and are in regular use. We hope that by the end of the year 2000, visitors to our Department will be able to access the database itself. Already, parts of the database have been adapted for use in the Museum's exhibition galleries.

CASUALTY LISTS AND ROLLS OF HONOUR

In addition to the set of the Commonwealth War Graves Commission memorial and cemetery registers, the Department of Printed Books holds a large collection of operational and shipping histories, some of which include casualties, and a number of published rolls of honour. Of particular importance for confirming basic details, are the volumes of the *Cross of Sacrifice* by S D and D B Jarvis, covering the First World War. The information these volumes contain includes full name, rank, decorations, cause of death, date of death, unit and details of grave or memorial location. The authors have also taken care to cross refer possible misspellings of names. Both the CWGC registers and the volumes by Jarvis are conveniently close to hand in our Reading Room.

Our library catalogues can also reveal a rich vein of privately produced rolls of honour for schools, universities, companies, professions and for localities. Of particular interest are the two typescript registers of *Merchant Navy Radio Officers Killed at Sea, 1939-1945*, compiled by Peter J Barber and George V Monk and the *Lloyd's War Losses* volumes which are compilations of shipping casualties drawn from the manuscript records held in the Lloyd's Marine Collection at the Guildhall Library. Also of note are the volumes of the *National Roll of the Great War, 1914-1918*. The volumes for Southampton and Portsmouth (Sections IV and X) in particular include references to Merchant Navy personnel. The National Roll project was never completed and is far from comprehensive. Paradoxically it can be both unreliable, but at times, an excellent source of personal information. Inclusion was by subscription and the individuals listed included many combatants who returned safely home at the end of the war.

The **National Inventory of War Memorials**, based at the Imperial War Museum, may be able to assist with enquiries relating to memorials to Merchant Navy personnel. The NIWM is an information-gathering project which aims to create a database of all known war memorials in the United Kingdom, estimated to be in the region of sixty thousand. Although individuals are not listed on the database, files containing additional material may be consulted by prior appointment. Please note that the National Inventory will welcome information on any memorial not already included.

Other Sources

Periodical publications, including 'old comrades' association newsletters, often carry information which will be of interest to the family history researcher. The Department of Printed Books can advise on those most relevant to a particular enquiry, but if several addresses are required, the researcher may wish to purchase a copy of our recently updated *List of Current Periodicals*.

In addition, there are many magazines on the market which offer advice and guidance on family history; one of which is *Family Tree Magazine*, published monthly by **Michael and Mary Armstrong, 61 Great Whyte, Ramsey, Huntingdon, Cambridgeshire PE17 1HL**.

Genealogical societies, such as the **Federation of Family History Societies, c/o Benson Room, Birmingham and Midland Institute, Margaret Street, Birmingham B3 3BS** and the **Society of Genealogists, 14 Charterhouse Buildings, Goswell Road, London EC1M 7BA** are also able to offer advice, as well as provide details of local societies and organisations. The Federation of Family History Societies publishes the semi-annual journal *Family History News and Digest*, while the Society of Genealogists publishes the quarterly journal *Genealogists Magazine*. Both societies have produced useful guides for the family historian, some of which are listed in Appendix IV.

The researcher will also find operational records, shipping company and individual ships' histories invaluable for background detail. The Department of Printed Books holds copies of the official histories *The Merchant Navy* by

Archibald Hurd, *Seaborne Trade* by C Ernest Fayle and *Naval Operations* by Julian S Corbett and Henry Newbolt, all of which give a good insight to maritime operations during the First World War. Facsimile reprints of the publications by C Ernest Fayle and Julian S Corbett are available for purchase direct from the Department of Printed Books. Although no specific 'official histories' have been produced for the Second World War the researcher will find the commercially published volumes *Life Line* by Peter Elphick, *Survivors* by G H and R Bennett and *The Fourth Service* by John Slader give excellent accounts of the varying roles of the Merchant Navy.

The most important, and perhaps the most complex area of the Merchant Navy's involvement in maritime operations revolves around the concept of the convoy. Here, the Department of Printed Books holds a wealth of published accounts relating to Atlantic, Arctic and Mediterranean convoys. A few examples have been listed in the Select Bibliography in Appendix IV. The definitive book on this subject is the newly published *The Allied Convoy System, 1939-1945: Organisation, Defence and Operation* by Arnold Hague, which researchers will find invaluable for tracing the movements and composition of all convoys in operation during the period of the Second World War. Also of particular interest is the privately published *SAWAS, 1939-1947 Book of Thanks* edited by Captain E A S Bailey, which lists the code numbers and sailing dates of all convoys sailing from the UK to South Africa, includes the names of the troopships and the escorting naval vessels involved and rolls of honour of the servicemen who perished during these voyages. This is a rare publication printed as a limited edition of only 700 copies. The researcher will also find that the multi-volume *The War at Sea: Preliminary Narrative*, an unpublished typescript compiled by the Admiralty Naval Staff during the Second World War, contains many useful references to individual convoys as well as to merchant shipping losses. Another good source of reference for convoy losses is *Axis Submarine Successes, 1939-1945* by Jurgen Rohwer. The Department of Printed Books has compiled select reading lists on the convoys by theatre. Copies of these lists are available on request.

Official documentation such as operational records, convoy records and ships' logs are held at the **Public Record Office, Ruskin Avenue, Kew, Richmond, Surrey TW9 4DU**. The most relevant files for operational records relating to the First World War, are the Ministry of Transport files *MT 23* and *MT 25*. Convoy records are to be found in the Admiralty files *ADM 137* and ships' logs in the Board of Trade files *BT 165*. Operational records relating to the Second World War are included in the Ministry of (War) Transport files *MT 40* and *MT 59* with convoy records in Admiralty files *ADM 199* (includes survivors' reports) and *ADM 237*. Ships' logs for the period are with the **Registry of Shipping and Seamen** but the researcher will find the **Guildhall Library's** collection of *Voyage Record Cards* invaluable.

Records of shipping companies are useful to the researcher as they contain information on the company's employees, as well as details of the fleet and the ships' sailings. The Department of Printed Books holds a good collection of shipping company histories and individual ships' histories although, in the main, they refer to the larger companies such as the Cunard Line, P & O and the Union-Castle line, famous vessels like the *SS Lusitania, SS Lancastria, Queen Elizabeth and Queen Mary*. However, there are many 'smaller' company histories as well as individual ships' histories published in periodicals such as *Sea Breezes: the Magazine of Ships and the Sea* (published by 'Sea Breezes,' Units 28-30, Spring Valley Industrial Estate,

Braddan, Isle of Man IM2 2QS) and *Marine News: Journal of the World Ship Society* (published by the World Ship Society, c/o the Membership Secretary Stan Hancock, 13 Headingley Close, Almond Hill, Stevenage, Hertfordshire SG1 3RU). Runs of these periodicals are available for consultation in our Reading Room.

Most of the official records relating to shipping companies have been lodged with the **National Maritime Museum**, the **Guildhall Library**, the **Merseyside Maritime Museum**, the **Glasgow University Archives**, the **Liverpool University Archives** and various other archives and record offices around the country. Details of some of these archives are listed in Appendix III.

The Department of Printed Books does not hold any detailed charts showing sailings or wreck positions other than those reproduced in published histories. Officially produced charts are held by the **Public Record Office** and the **National Maritime Museum**. In addition, accurate locations for wrecks, particularly off the UK coastlines, may be obtained from the **Ministry of Defence, Hydrographic Office, Admiralty Way, Taunton, Somerset TA1 2DN**. A search fee may be levied.

Researchers may also be interested in the records of seamen's trade unions, as they too contain some useful references to the seaman's career. Records of the **National Union of Seamen** from 1911 and some branch records of the **British Seafarers' Union**, from 1915, are to be found in the archives of the **University of Warwick, Modern Records Centre, University Library, Gibbet Hill Road, Coventry CV4 7AL**.

The Department of Printed Books holds a fair collection of complementary published sources, including titles giving technical background to the ships, armament and training involved, as well as badges, uniforms and medals. We hold runs of the *Lloyd's Register of Shipping* (1914-1940) and the *Mercantile Navy List* (1913-1966). Although incomplete they do help to establish basic facts about individual ships. Periodicals and our collection of autobiographies can also provide unexpected references on differing areas of service with the Merchant Navy.

Researchers are welcome to use the full range of archival and research material available at the **Imperial War Museum**. These include materials held by the Departments of Art, Documents, Exhibits and Firearms and the Film and Video, Photograph, and Sound Archives.

The Department of Documents in particular, holds a number of unpublished diaries and memoirs written by officers and crew who served in the Merchant Navy during the First and Second World Wars. A few give a full account of their experiences at sea, but the majority are specifically concerned either with the sinking of their vessel, their capture by the enemy or their participation in particular convoys and other maritime operations.

Similar collections are held by the Sound Archive. Their collection of interviews with veterans offer an "array of experience often recalled with emotional force." In many cases the Photograph Archive can produce a print of an individual ship. Although there are many photographs of merchant seamen, the views tend to be of groups rather than individual portraits.

An access guide to all the collections is available on request.

For information relating to the 19th Century and earlier, we would recommend contacting the **National Maritime Museum**, the **Guildhall Library** and the **Merseyside Maritime Museum**. Details of these and other relevant museums and archives are outlined in Appendix III.

Appendix I

REGISTRATION OF SHIPPING AND SEAMEN

The registration of seamen was originally the responsibility of the Admiralty. From the late 17th Century several unsuccessful attempts were made to set up a Register of Seamen until in 1835, the Merchant Seamen Act established the **General Register Office of Merchant Seamen** under the control of the Admiralty at the London Customs House. The Register was intended to allow the Admiralty to select seamen to man the Royal Navy in times of war. It did not include fishermen at this time.

The 1872 Merchant Shipping Act saw the establishment of the **Registrar General of Shipping and Seamen** which, by 1888, had five divisions concerned with the registration of shipping; the Royal Naval Reserve, Masters, Mates and Engineers, ships' employment and general service records. In 1939, the control of the Registrar General of Shipping and Seamen was transferred from the Board of Trade to the Ministry of Shipping and then, in 1941, to its successor the Ministry of War Transport. In 1946 it became part of the Marine Crews Division of the Ministry of Transport, returned to the Board of Trade in 1965 and was absorbed into the Department of Trade and Industry in 1970. In 1992 it became part of the Marine Safety Agency and was renamed the **Registry of Shipping and Seamen**.

Following the passing of the 1835 Merchant Seamen Act, Masters of ships were required to file Crew Lists and Agreements with the new General Register Office of Merchant Seamen. (From 1835 to date there have been six Registers created). In 1910 an Advisory Committee on Merchant Shipping proposed the creation of a Central Index Register of Seamen to the Board of Trade. This Fourth Register was started in 1913 and continued until 1940.

The Register contains individual records of all categories of persons who went to sea, including some women, but not Masters who were recorded in separate Registers. These records are filed in alphabetical order by name, and record the date of birth, rank, details of ships on which served, date of joining (engagement) and date of leaving (discharge).

In 1941, the Essential Work (Merchant Navy) created a Merchant Navy Reserve Pool. To ensure that seamen would always be available to man vessels, the Government paid them to remain in the Reserve Pool when they were ashore. Therefore, since continuous pay was available, an efficient Register of Seamen became possible. All those who had served at sea during the previous five years were required to register with the Registrar of Shipping and Seamen. This led to the formation of the Fifth Register of Seamen which was maintained until 1972.

Until the Merchant Shipping (Fishing Boats) Act of 1883, information relating to fishermen and fishing vessels was included in the general run of Merchant Shipping and Seamen's records. However, the new Act decreed that Skippers of fishing vessels had to enter into an agreement with every seaman carried to sea from any port in the United Kingdom. These Crew Lists and Agreements were filed separately.

Until 1845 there was no system for the registration of officers (Masters, Mates, Engineers and Cooks) until the Registrar General of Shipping and Seamen started to compile an alphabetical Register of Masters from information contained in the filed Crew Lists, but this was short lived. At the same time a system of examinations was introduced for Masters and Mates. At first it was voluntary and applied only to those on 'foreign trade' vessels. This was extended to those on 'home trade' vessels in 1854. The taking of the examinations became compulsory in 1850; a system which continues to the present day. However, those judged by the examiners to have sufficient experience as a Master or Mate and those retiring from the Royal Navy were eligible, without formal examination, for Certificates of Service. Those without sufficient service, and those wishing to progress in the ranks were granted Certificates of Competency on passing examinations.

These Certificates were entered into Registers arranged in numerical order and by type of trade i.e., foreign and home. They detailed the name, date and place of birth, rank examined for, or served in, and date of the issue of the Certificate. Information on a Master or Mate's voyage, after the Certificate was granted, and in some cases details of death, injuries and previous vessels on which they served, were included. The system of recording the issue of Certificates changed in 1913.

Lloyd's Captains' Registers contain details of Masters active between 1869 and 1948. They are arranged alphabetically and list all holders of the Masters' Certificates. They give the full name, date and place of birth as well as the Certificate number and date and place of examination. Included is a complete history of the Master's career, giving the names of the vessels on which he served, in what capacity i.e. Master or Mate, and the general area of service. These entries are based on the details supplied to Lloyds by the Registrar General of Shipping and Seamen.

Certification of Engineers began in 1862 along the same lines as described above i.e. they could obtain their Certificates as a result of examination (Certificates of Competency) or by exemption due to long service (Certificates of Service). Similarly the Merchant Shipping Act of 1906 called for the registration of Cooks which began in 1908.

Certification of Skippers and Mates (or Second Hands) of fishing vessels began in 1884, extending the system which had been applied to Masters and Mates. From 1910 a combined index to Certificates of Competency for Masters, Mates, Engineers and Fishing Officers for Home and Foreign Trade was introduced.

The Registration of Shipping was made compulsory by the Shipping and Navigation Act of 1786 which established the **Registrar General of Shipping** under the Board of Customs. The Merchant Shipping Act of 1854 transferred the general supervision of matters relating to merchant ships to the Board of Trade. These Acts decreed that all owners of British vessels had to register details of the vessel and changes of ownership. The information submitted included the official number, name and port of vessel, British or foreign built, sailing or steam, where and when built, construction details, tonnage and the name and address of the owner and/or manager. The official number became the main means of reference to a vessel. The name could be changed and the vessel re-registered but the number remained constant, even if the vessel was sold abroad and then returned to British ownership.

In 1890 a new system was introduced so that all papers relating to a ship's registration were kept together until the registry of the vessel ceased. These papers were then filed under the date of the vessel's de-registration.

In 1894 the Merchant Shipping Act decreed that every fishing vessel was also to be lettered and numbered, have official papers and be entered on a separate Register.

From 1850 Masters were required to keep a *Ship's Log*. These Logs are a record of a period of time in the life of a vessel. It is divided up into two sections:

The *Tabular Section* which records all the voyages and the ports at which the vessel docked. Births, marriages and deaths, of crew and passengers on board were also recorded with more general administrative matters. The Log will usually give the vessel's position and time of these events. Although sailing and arrival dates and times are sometimes given, they were not officially required.

The *Narrative Section* contains written entries concerning other events which occur on each voyage. These include accidents and illnesses among crew members, and any passengers, disciplinary matters and often a seaman's conduct record.

Appendix II

ABBREVIATIONS

These are a selection only of the most commonly used abbreviations. The Department of Printed Books holds several published guides to abbreviations in use at various times during the 20th Century.

General

ADM	Admiralty
BT	Board of Trade
BSU	British Seafarers' Union
CAM	Catapult Aircraft Merchantman
CS	Continuous Service
CWGC	Commonwealth War Graves Commission
DEMS	Defensively Equipped Merchant Ships
HM	His Majesty's/Her Majesty's
IWGC	Imperial War Graves Commission
LR	Lloyd's Register
MAC	Merchant ship Aircraft Carrier
MOD	Ministry of Defence
MM	Mercantile Marine/Merchant Marine
MN	Merchant Navy
MNL	Mercantile Navy List
MS	Merchant Service
MT	Ministry of (War) Transport
MV	Motor Vessel
PRO	Public Record Office
RFA	Royal Fleet Auxiliary
RGSS	Registrar General of Shipping and Seamen
RN	Royal Navy/Royal Naval

RND	Royal Naval Division
RNR	Royal Naval Reserve
RNR(T)	Royal Naval Reserve Trawler Section
RNVR	Royal Naval Volunteer Reserve
RSS	Registry of Shipping and Seamen
SS	Steamship/Sailing Ship

Ranks and Titles

A	Apprentice
AB	Able Seaman
AS	Assistant Steward
B	Boatswain (Bo'sun)
C	Captain
Cd	Commissioned
Cdre	Commodore
Cf M	Chief Mate
Ck	Cook
Cdt	Cadet
CE	Chief Engineer
Cr	Carpenter
CS	Chief Steward
F	Fireman
Gr	Gunner
M	Mate
2M	Second Mate
3M	Third Mate
MO	Medical Officer
Mr	Master
OS	Ordinary Seaman
P	Purser
QM	Quartermaster
S	Seaman

Sg	Surgeon
Skr	Skipper
Sl Mr	Sailmaker
St	Stoker
Tr	Trimmer
WO	Wireless Operator
WTO	Wireless Telegraphy Operator

Honours and Awards

AM	Albert Medal
AM(B)	Albert Medal in Bronze
AM(G)	Albert Medal in Gold
BEM	British Empire Medal
BEM(Gall)	British Empire Medal (specifically for gallantry)
CB	Companion of the Order of the Bath
CBE	Commander of the Order of the British Empire
Commendn	Commendation
DSC	Distinguished Service Cross
DSM	Distinguished Service Medal
DSO	Distinguished Service Order
EGM	Empire Gallantry Medal
GC	George Cross
GM	George Medal
KBE	Knight Commander of the Order of the British Empire
KCB	Knight Commander of the Order of the Bath
KG	Knight of the Order of the Garter
LlBvymed	Lloyd's War Medal for Bravery at Sea
LlLfSvymed	Lloyd's Medal for Saving Life at Sea

LlMerSvmed	Lloyd's Medal for Meritorious Service
MBE	Member of the Order of the British Empire
MBE(Gall)	Member of the Order of the British Empire (specifically for gallantry)
MID	Mention-in-Despatches
OBE	Officer of the Order of the British Empire
RRC	Member of the Order of the Royal Red Cross
RRC Bar	Bar to the Royal Red Cross
SGM Br	Board of Trade Bronze Medal for Saving Life at Sea
VC	Victoria Cross

Appendix III

ADDRESSES

Listed below are details of some museums, archives and record offices which may be able to offer assistance with family history enquiries. Please note that it is always advisable to contact an institution in advance of an intended visit in order to check on the availability of material relating to your particular enquiry and confirm opening hours. Those with internet access will find that many institutions now have their own website which outline their holdings, arrangements for public access and details of any search fees and/or charges which may be levied. Information on other museums and archives are to be found in the annual publications the *World of Learning* and the *Museums Yearbook*, available at most libraries and information centres. ASLIB, in collaboration with the Museums Association, also publishes the very useful *Directory of Museums and Special Collections in the United Kingdom*.

RECORD OFFICES AND GENEALOGY

Bristol Record Office
'B' Bond Warehouse, Smeaton Road, Bristol BS1 6XN
Tel: 0117 922 4224
Website: http://www.bristol-city.gov.uk/recordoffice

Commonwealth War Graves Commission
2 Marlow Road, Maidenhead, Berkshire SL6 7DX
Tel: 01628 634221
Website: http://www.cwgc.org

Family Records Centre
1 Myddelton Street, London EC1R 1UW
Tel: 020 8392 5300
Website: http://www.pro.gov.uk

Family Tree Magazine
61 Great Whyte, Ramsey, Huntingdon,
Cambridgeshire PE17 1HL
Tel: 01487 814050
Website: http://www.family-tree.co.uk

Federation of Family History Societies
The Benson Room, Birmingham and Midland Institute,
Margaret Street, Birmingham B3 3BS
Website: http://www.ffhs.org.uk

General Register Office (Dublin)
Joyce House, 8-11 Lombard Street East, Dublin 2, Eire
Tel: 01 6711000

General Register Office (Northern Ireland)
Oxford House, 49-55 Chichester Street, Belfast BT1 4HL,
Northern Ireland
Tel: 028 9025 2021
Website: http://www.nisra.gov.uk

General Register Office for Scotland
New Register House, 3 West Register Street,
Edinburgh EH1 3YT, Scotland
Tel: 0131 314 4450
Website: http://www.gro-scotland.gov.uk/

Ministry of Defence, DR(2)A Navy
Bourne Avenue, Hayes, Middlesex UB3 1RF

Ministry of Defence, Honours and Awards
Room 115, Victory Building, HM Naval Base,
Portsmouth, Hampshire PO1 3LS

Ministry of Defence, Hydrographic Office
Admiralty Way, Taunton, Somerset TA1 2DN
Tel: 01823 337900
Website: http://www.ukho.gov.uk

Ministry of Defence, NPP(ACS)1E Centurion Building
Grange Road, Gosport, Hampshire, PO1 9XA

National Archives of Ireland
Bishop Street, Dublin 8, Eire
Tel: 01 4072300
Website: http://www.nationalarchives.ie

National Archives of Scotland
HM General Register House,
Edinburgh EH1 3YY, Scotland
Tel: 0131 535 1314

Public Record Office
Ruskin Avenue, Kew, Richmond, Surrey TW9 4DU
Tel: 020 8392 5200
Website: http://www.pro.gov.uk

Public Record Office of Northern Ireland
66 Balmoral Avenue, Belfast BT9 6NY, Northern Ireland
Tel: 028 9025 1318
Website: http://www.nics.gov.uk

Registry of Shipping and Seamen
Anchor House, Cheviot Close, Parc-ty-Glas,
Llanishen, Cardiff CF4 5JA

Society of Genealogists
14 Charterhouse Buildings, Goswell Road,
London EC1M 7BA
Tel: 020 7251 8799
Website: http://www.sog.org.uk

MUSEUMS, LIBRARIES AND ARCHIVES

Bristol City Museum
Queens Road, Bristol BS8 1RL
Tel: 0117 922 3571
Website: http://www.bristol-city.gov.uk

British Library, Newspaper Library
Colindale Avenue, London NW9 5HE
Tel: 020 7412 7353
Website: http://portico.bl.uk/collections/newspapers

British Library, Oriental and India Office Collections
96 Euston Road, London NW1 2DB
Tel: 020 7412 7873
Website: http://portico.bl.uk/
(records of the East India Company and some Merchant Navy
personnel)

Department of Transport, Marine Library
105 Commercial Road, Southampton SO1 0ZD
Tel: 023 8032 9100

Glasgow City Archives

Mitchell Library, North Street, Glasgow G3 7DN

Tel: 0141 287 2910

Website: http://www.glasgow.gov.uk/gcl/home.htm

(records of some local shipping companies e.g. Elder
Dempster Line)

Glasgow University Archives and Business Record Centre

13 Thurso Street, Glasgow G11 6PE

Tel: 0141 330 5515

Website: http://www.archives.gla.ac.uk

(records of some local shipping companies e.g.
Anchor Line and Ellerman Line)

Guildhall Library, Lloyd's Marine Collection

Aldermanbury, London EC2P 2EJ

Tel: 020 7332 1868

Website: http://www.cityoflondon.gov.uk/search-guildhall

Hartlepool Museum Service

Sir William Gray House, Clarence Road, Hartlepool TS24 8BT

Tel: 01429 523438

Hull Maritime Museum

Queen Victoria Square, Hull HU1 3DX

Tel: 01482 613902

Website: http://www.hullcc.gov.uk

Liverpool University

Special Collections and Archives, Sydney Jones Library,
University of Liverpool, PO Box 123, Liverpool L69 3DA

Tel: 0151 794 2696

Website: http://www.liv.ac.uk

(records of local shipping companies e.g. Cunard)

Lloyd's Register of Shipping
71 Fenchurch Street, London EC3M 4BS
Tel: 020 7709 9166
Website: http://www.lr.org/

Lowestoft Maritime Museum
Sparrows Nest Gardens, Whapload Road, Lowestoft,
Suffolk NR32 1XT
Tel: 01502 561963

Marine Society
202 Lambeth Road, London SE1 7JW
Tel: 020 7261 9535
Website: http://www.marine-society.org

Maritime History Archive
Memorial University of Newfoundland, St John's,
Newfoundland, A1C 5S7, Canada
Website: http://www.mun.ca/library/colldev/mhg/index.html

Merseyside Maritime Museum
Archives and Library, Albert Dock, Liverpool L3 4AA
Tel: 0151 478 4424
Website: http://www.nmgm.org.uk

National Library of Wales
Aberystwyth, Ceredigion SY23 3BU, Wales
Tel: 01970 623800
Website: http://www.llgc.org.uk

National Maritime Museum
Romney Road, Greenwich, London SE10 9NF
Tel: 020 8858 4422
Website: http://www.nmm.ac.uk

National Register of Archives
Quality House, Quality Court, Chancery Lane,
London WC2A 1HP
Tel: 020 7242 1198
(for locations of archives and special collections)

Shipwreck and Marine Ltd.
Ropewalk House, Charlestown, Cornwall PL25 3NN
Tel: 01726 73104
(for index and location of shipwrecks around UK Coastline)

Warwick University
Modern Records Centre, University Library, University of
Warwick, Coventry CV4 7AL
Tel: 024 7652 4219
Website: http://www.warwick.ac.uk
(records of Merchant Seamen's trade unions)

ADDITIONAL WEBSITES

Ships
Website: http://www.ships.co.uk/informat.htm
(includes details of some sources of historical records
about ships and maritime subjects in the UK).

Records of British Seamen and Ships
Website: http://www.ukans.edu/~kansite/ww_one/naval/sdata
001.htm
(short but useful list of references).

International Maritime Ring
Website: http://www.webring.org/cgi-bin/webring?ring=mar-
itimering;list
(contains a large number of useful links to all aspects of the
world's merchant navies and their ships).

Appendix IV

SELECT BIBLIOGRAPHY

Below are listed a selection of published sources and material held by the Department of Printed Books. These may be consulted in our reading room by prior appointment; please give at least 24 hours notice of arrival. In addition, specific subject bibliographies and information sheets are available on request. Please note that we have not attempted to list the many periodical titles that are relevant to maritime research, but we are happy to advise on specific titles where applicable.

Many of these recommended publications will also be available through your local public library or bookseller and in the case of the 'out of print' volumes through second-hand and specialist dealers.

For ease of use, the list has been broken down into the following main subject areas to reflect the different sections in this booklet: Genealogy and Family History (p. 60); Service Records and Archival Guides (p. 61); Medals and Awards (p. 63); Casualties and Rolls of Honour (p. 65); Maritime Operations in the 20th Century (p. 69); Merchant Shipping Companies and their Ships (p. 75); Life in the Merchant Navy (p. 79).

GENEALOGY AND FAMILY HISTORY

AMSDEN, Peter C.

Basic approach to ... Making Contact with Relatives by Peter C. Amsden.

Federation of Family History Societies, Bury, Lancs., 1999.

ISBN 1-86006-099-4 (pbk.)

COX, Jane

Never been here before?: a Genealogist's Guide to the Family Records Centre by Jane Cox and Stella Colwell.

Public Record Office, Richmond, Surrey, 1997.

(Public Record Office Readers' Guide; no. 17)

ISBN 1-873162-41-3 (pbk.)

COX, Jane

New to Kew? by Jane Cox.

Public Record Office, Richmond, Surrey, 1997.

(Public Record Office Readers' Guide; no. 16)

ISBN 1-873162-40-5 (pbk.)

COX, Jane

Tracing your Ancestors in the Public Record Office by Jane Cox and Timothy Padfield.

5th edition by Amanda Bevan; Public Record Office, Richmond, Surrey, 1998.

(Public Record Office Handbook; no. 19)

ISBN 1-873162-61-8 (pbk.)

GIBBONS, Lilian

Basic facts about ... Using Death and Burial Records for Family Historians by Lilian Gibbons.

Federation of Family History Societies, Bury, Lancashire, 1999.

ISBN 1-86006-102-8 (pbk.)

PUBLIC RECORD OFFICE

Record Repositories in Great Britain by the
Public Record Office.
Public Record Office, Richmond, Surrey and the Royal
Commission on Historical Manuscripts, London, 1997.
ISBN 1-873162-40-5 (pbk.)

SERVICE RECORDS AND ARCHIVAL GUIDES

BARRISKILL, D.T.

*A Guide to the Lloyd's Marine Collection and Related Marine
Sources at the Guildhall Library* compiled by D.T. Barriskill.
Guildhall Library, London, 1994.
(Guildhall Library Research Guide; 7)
ISBN 0-900422-37-8 (pbk.)

CANTWELL, J.D.

*The Second World War: a Guide to Documents in the Public
Record Office* by J.D. Cantwell.
2nd edition; Public Record Office, Richmond, Surrey, 1998.
(Public Record Office Handbook; no. 15)
ISBN 1-873162-60-X (pbk.)

FOSTER, Janet

*British Archives: a Guide to Archive Resources in the United
Kingdom* by Janet Foster and Julia Sheppard.
[Rev. ed.]; Macmillan, London, 1995.
ISBN 0-333-532-554

HARVEY, Richard

A Guide to Genealogical Sources in Guildhall Library
compiled by Richard Harvey.
Guildhall Library, London, 1997.
(Guildhall Library Research Guide; 1)
ISBN 0-900422-41-6 (pbk.)

HOGG, Peter L.
Basic Facts about ... Using Merchant Ship Records for Family Historians by Peter L. Hogg.
Federation of Family History Societies, Bury, Lancashire, 1999.
ISBN 1-86006-045-5 (pbk.)

IMPERIAL WAR MUSEUM
Tracing Your Family History: Royal Navy.
Imperial War Museum, London, 1999.
ISBN 1-901623-36-X (pbk.)

PUBLIC RECORD OFFICE
The series of information leaflets already referred to in the main text is available on the Internet. The following titles are a few examples of the material produced.

Merchant Shipping: Crew Lists and Agreements after 1861. (Domestic Records Information Sheet; no. 91)

Merchant Seamen: Registers of Service, 1913-1941. (Domestic Records Information Sheet; no. 90)

Records of the Registrar General of Shipping and Seamen. (Records Information Leaflet; no. 50)

Ships' Passenger Lists, 1878-1960. (Domestic Records Information Sheet; no. 56)

SMITH, Kelvin
Records of Merchant Shipping and Seamen by Kelvin Smith, Christopher T. Watts and Michael J. Watts.
Public Record Office, Richmond, Surrey, 1998.
ISBN 1-873-162-49-9 (pbk.)

WATTS, Christopher T.
My Ancestor was a Merchant Seamen: How can I Find out More about Him? by Christopher T. Watts and Michael J. Watts.
Society of Genealogists, London, 1987.
ISBN 0-901878-73-1 (pbk.)

MEDALS AND AWARDS

ABBOTT, P.E.
British Gallantry Awards by P.E. Abbott and J.M.A. Tamplin.
Nimrod Dix, London, 1981.
ISBN 0-85112-173-X

BROWN, George A.
Lloyd's War Medal for Bravery at Sea by George A. Brown.
Western Canadian Distributors, Langley,
British Columbia, 1992.
ISBN 0-94813-65-5 [sic]

DICKSON, Bill Chatterton
Seedie's List of Awards to the Merchant Navy for World War II compiled by Bill Chatterton Dickson.
Ripley Registers, Tisbury, Wiltshire, 1997.
ISBN 0-9513380-4-8

DICKSON, Bill Chatterton
Seedie's Roll of Naval Honours and Awards, 1939-1959 compiled by Bill Chatterton Dickson.
Ripley Registers, Tisbury, Wiltshire, 1989.
ISBN 0-9513380-0-5

DORLING, H. Taprell
Ribbons and Medals by H. Taprell Dorling; edited and revised by Alec A. Purves.
Osprey, London, 1983.
ISBN 0-85045-516-2

DYMOND, Steve
Researching British Military Medals: a Practical Guide by Steve Dymond.
Crowood Press, Marlborough, Wiltshire, 1999.
ISBN 1-86126-282-5

FEVYER, W.H.
The Distinguished Service Cross, 1901-1938 by W.H. Fevyer.
Stamp Exchange, London, 1991.
ISBN 0-948130-63-6

FEVYER, W.H.
The Distinguished Service Medal, 1914-1920 compiled by W.H. Fevyer.
Hayward, London, 1982.
ISBN 0-903754-97-5

FEVYER, W.H.
The Distinguished Service Medal, 1939-1946 compiled by W.H. Fevyer.
Hayward, London, 1981.
ISBN 0-903754-90-8

GOULD, Robert W.
British Campaign Medals: Waterloo to the Gulf by Robert W. Gould.
Arms and Armour Press, London, 1994.
ISBN 1-85409-224-3

PUBLIC RECORD OFFICE

First World War: Indexes to Medal Entitlement.
(Records Information Leaflet; no. 105)

Records of Medals.
(Records Information Leaflet; no. 108)

The Register of the George Cross.
This England Books, Cheltenham, 1985.
ISBN 0-906324-06-8

The Register of the Victoria Cross.
Rev. ed.; This England Books, Cheltenham, 1988.
ISBN 0-906324-07-6

SCARLETT, R.J.

Under Hazardous Circumstances: a Register of Awards of
Lloyd's War Medal for Bravery at Sea, 1939-1945 by R.J.
Scarlett.
Naval and Military Press, Dallington, Sussex, 1992.
ISBN 0-948130-49-0

CASUALTIES AND ROLLS OF HONOUR

SHIPS' LOSSES

British Vessels Lost at Sea, 1914-18 and 1939-45: [facsimile
reprint of four HMSO publications ...]
Patrick Stephens, Wellingborough, Northants., 1988.
ISBN 1-85260-134-5

HOCKING, Charles
Dictionary of Disasters at Sea during the Age of Steam ...
1824-1962 [2 volumes] by Charles Hocking.
Lloyd's, London, 1969.

HOOKE, Norman
Modern Shipping Disasters, 1963-1987 by Norman Hooke.
Lloyd's, London, 1989.
ISBN 1-85044-211-8

Lloyd's War Losses: the First World War: Casualties to
Shipping through Enemy Causes, 1914-1918.
Lloyd's, London, 1990.
ISBN 1-85044-314-9

Lloyd's War Losses: the Second World War. Volume I: British,
Allied and Neutral Merchant Vessels Sunk or Destroyed by War
Causes.
Lloyd's, London, 1989.
ISBN 1-85044-314-9

Lloyd's War Losses: the Second World War. Volume II:
Statistics, Vessels Disappeared, Losses, Without Trace, Badly
Damaged, Naval Losses, British, Allied and Neutral Warship
Losses, Vessels Sunk by Mines after the War.
Lloyd's, London, 1991.
ISBN 1-85044-412-9

Lloyd's War Losses: the Second World War. Volume III: Vessels
Lost or Damaged by War Causes while under Control of
German, Italian or other European Axis Powers [2 parts].
[Lloyd's, London], n.d.

PUBLIC RECORD OFFICE
Records relating to Shipwrecks.
(Records Information Leaflet; no. 65)

TENNANT, A.J.

British Merchant Ships Sunk by U-Boats in the 1914-1918 War by A.J. Tennant.

Starling Press, Newport, Gwent, 1990.

ISBN 0-9516314-0-3 (pbk.)

WILLIAMS, David

Wartime Disasters at Sea: every Passenger Ship Loss in World War I and II by David Williams.

Patrick Stephens, Yeovil, Somerset, 1997.

ISBN 1-85260-565-0

YOUNG, John M.

Britain's Sea War: a Diary of Ship Losses, 1939-1945 by John M. Young.

Patrick Stephens, Wellingborough, Northants., 1989.

ISBN 1-85260-042-X

MEMORIALS

GIBSON, Edwin

Courage Remembered: the Story Behind the Construction and Maintenance of the Commonwealth Military Cemeteries and Memorials of the Wars of 1914-1918 and 1939-1945 by Edwin Gibson and G. Kingsley Ward.

HMSO, London, 1989.

ISBN 0-11-772608-7

SAUNDERS, David

Britain's Maritime Memorials and Mementoes by David Saunders.

Patrick Stephens, Sparkford, Somerset, 1996.

ISBN 1-85260-466-2

BARBER, Peter J.
British and Commonwealth Radio Officers of the British Merchant Marine Lost at Sea, 1939-1945: Complete Alphabetical and Ship Register compiled by Peter J. Barber and George V. Monk.
[N. pub., n.p.], 1998.

BARBER, Peter J.
Memorial-Register: British Merchant Navy Radio Officers Killed at Sea, 1939-1945 by Peter J. Barber.
[P.J. Barber, n.p., 1990].

JARVIS, S.D.
Cross of Sacrifice, Volume 2: Officers who Died in the Service of the Royal Navy, Royal Naval Reserve, Royal Naval Volunteer Reserve, Royal Marines, Royal Naval Air Service and Royal Air Force, 1914-1919 by S.D. Jarvis and D.B. Jarvis.
Roberts Medals, Reading, Berkshire, 1993
ISBN 1-873058-31-4

JARVIS, S.D.
Cross of Sacrifice, Volume 4: Non-commissioned Officers and Men of the Royal Navy, Royal Flying Corps and Royal Air Force, 1914 - 1919 by S.D. Jarvis and D.B. Jarvis.
Roberts Medals, Reading, Berkshire, 1996.
ISBN 1-873058-41-1

JARVIS, S.D.
Cross of Sacrifice, Volume 5: the Officers, Men and Women of the Merchant Navy and Mercantile Fleet Auxiliary, 1914-1919 by S.D. Jarvis and D.B. Jarvis.
Roberts Medals, Reading, Berkshire, [date to be announced]
ISBN 1-873058-41-2

National Roll of the Great War, 1914-1918: Sections I-VII, IX-X, XII-XIII
National Publishing, London, [1920-1922?].
(incomplete set held by the Department of Printed Books)

MEDICAL

MELLOR, W. Franklin
Casualties and Medical Statistics edited by W. Franklin Mellor.
HMSO, London, 1972.
(History of the Second World War United Kingdom Medical Series)
ISBN 0-11-320997-5

MITCHELL, T.J.
Medical Services: Casualties and Medical Statistics of the Great War by T.J. Mitchell.
HMSO, London, 1931.
(History of the Great War Based on official documents)
[The Imperial War Museum, Department of Printed Books produced a reprint of this volume in 1997. ISBN 1-870423-28-3]

MARITIME OPERATIONS IN THE 20TH CENTURY

GENERAL

ALBION, Robert Greenhalgh
Naval and Maritime History: an Annotated Bibliography by Robert Greenhalgh Albion.
4th ed.; David and Charles, Newton Abbot, Devon, 1973.
ISBN 0-7153-6007-8

DOUGHTY, Martin
Merchant Shipping and War: a Study in Defence Planning in Twentieth-Century Britain by Martin Doughty.
Royal Historical Society, London, 1982.
ISBN 0-901050-83-0

HOPE, Ronald
The Merchant Navy by Ronald Hope.
Stanford Maritime, London, 1980.
ISBN 0-540-07335-0

LABAREE, Benjamin Woods
A Supplement (1971-1986) to Robert G. Albion's Naval and Maritime History: an Annotated Bibliography by Benjamin W. Labaree.
4th ed.; Mystic Seaport Museum, Mystic, Connecticut, 1988.
ISBN 0-913372-46-3 (pbk.)

WARNER, Oliver
The Life-Boat Service: a History of the Royal National Life-Boat Institution, 1824-1974 by Oliver Warner.
Cassell, London, 1974.
ISBN 0-304-29061-0

WEBB, William
Coastguard!: an Official History of HM Coastguard by William Webb.
HMSO, London, 1976.
ISBN 0-11-510675-8

CORBETT, Julian S.

Naval Operations [5 volumes and 4 map cases] by Julian S. Corbett and Henry Newbolt.

Longmans, Green, London, [1921-1931].

(History of the Great War Based on Official Documents)

[The Imperial War Museum, Department of Printed Books produced reprints of these volumes between 1995 and 1997.]

FAYLE, C. Ernest

Seaborne Trade [3 volumes] by C. Ernest Fayle.

John Murray, London, [1920-1924].

(History of the Great War Based on Official Documents)

[The Imperial War Museum, Department of Printed Books produced a reprint of these volumes in 1997.]

GIBSON, R.H.

The German Submarine War, 1914-1918 by R.H. Gibson and Maurice Prendergast.

Constable, London, 1931.

HURD, Archibald

The Merchant Navy [3 volumes] by Archibald Hurd.

John Murray, London, [1921-1929].

(History of the Great War Based on Official Documents)

ADMIRALTY. NAVAL STAFF. TORPEDO AND STAFF DUTIES DIVISION

The War at Sea, September 1939-September 1945: Preliminary Narrative compiled by the Admiralty, Naval Staff, Torpedo and Staff Duties Division.

[Admiralty, London, 1944-1946]

BEHRENS, C.B.A.

Merchant Shipping and the Demands of War by C.B.A. Behrens.

HMSO, London, 1955.

(History of the Second World War United Kingdom Civil Series)

ELPHICK, Peter

Life Line: the Merchant Navy at War, 1939-45 by Peter Elphick.

Chatham Publishing, London, 1999.

ISBN 1-86176-100-7

HAY, Doddy

War Under the Red Ensign: the Merchant Navy, 1939-45 by Doddy Hay.

Jane's, London, 1982.

ISBN 0-7106-0205-7

ROHWER, Jurgen

Axis Submarine Successes, 1939-1945 by Jurgen Rohwer.

Patrick Stephens, Cambridge, 1983.

ISBN 0-85059-695-5

ROSKILL, S.W.

The War at Sea, 1939-1945 [4 volumes] by S.W. Roskill.
HMSO, London, [1954-1961].
(History of the Second World War United Kingdom Military Series)
[The Imperial War Museum, Department of Printed Books produced a reprint of volume III, part II in 1995]

SLADER, John

The Fourth Service: Merchantmen at War, 1939-1945 by John Slader.
Robert Hale, London, 1994.
ISBN 0-7090-4848-3

CONVOYS

BAILEY, E.A.S.

SAWAS, 1939-1947: Book of Thanks, 1980 [3 volumes] edited by Captain E.A.S. Bailey ... [et al].
E.A.S. Bailey, Inversanda, Ardgour, by Fort William, 1981-1983.
ISBN 0-9507481-0-2

EDWARDS, Bernard

Attack and Sink!: the Battle for Convoy SC.42 by Bernard Edwards.
New Guild, Wimborne Minster, Dorset, 1995.
ISBN 1-89969-440-4 (pbk.)

HAGUE, Arnold

The Allied Convoy System, 1939-1945: Organisation, Defence and Operation by Arnold Hague.
Chatham Publishing, London, 2000
ISBN 1-55125-003-0

HAGUE, Arnold
Convoy Rescue Ships: a History of the Rescue Service, its Ships and their Crews, 1940-1945 by Arnold Hague.
World Ship Society, Gravesend, Kent, 1998.
ISBN 0-90-5617-88-6 (pbk.)

HASKELL, W.A.
Shadows on the Horizon: the Battle of Convoy HX-233 by W.A. Haskell.
Chatham Publishing, London, 1998.
ISBN 1-86176-081-7

MIDDLEBROOK, Martin
Convoy: the Battle for Convoy SC.122 and HX.229 by Martin Middlebrook.
Allen Lane, London, 1976.
ISBN 0-7139-0927-7

SMITH, Peter C.
Arctic Victory: the Story of Convoy PQ.18 by Peter C. Smith.
Kimber, London, 1975.
ISBN 0-7183-0074-2

SMITH, Peter C.
Pedestal: the Malta Convoy of August 1942 by Peter C. Smith.
2nd rev. ed.; Kimber, London, 1987.
ISBN 0-7183-0632-5

THOMAS, David A.
The Atlantic Star, 1939-1945 by David A. Thomas.
W.H. Allen, London, 1990.
ISBN 1-85227-147-7

THOMAS, David A.
Malta Convoys, 1940-42: the Struggle at Sea by David A. Thomas.
Leo Cooper, Barnsley, South Yorkshire, 1999.
ISBN 0-85052-663-9

WINTON, John
Convoy: the Defence of Sea Trade, 1890-1990 by John Winton.
Michael Joseph, London, 1983.
ISBN 0-7181-2163-5

WOODMAN, Richard
The Arctic Convoys, 1941-1945 by Richard Woodman.
John Murray, London, 1994.
ISBN 0-7195-5079-3

MERCHANT SHIPPING COMPANIES AND THEIR SHIPS

SHIPPING COMPANIES

COWDEN, James E.
The Price of Peace: Elder Dempster, 1939-1945 by James E. Cowden.
Jocast, Liverpool, 1981.
ISBN 0-9507480-0-5 (pbk.)

HEATON, P.M.
The Abbey Line: History of a Cardiff Shipping Venture by P.M. Heaton.
P.M. Heaton, Pontypool, Gwent, 1983.
ISBN 0-950-7714-2-2

HOWARTH, David
The Story of P and O: the Peninsular and Oriental Steam Navigation Company by David Howarth and Stephen Howarth.
Weidenfeld and Nicolson, London, 1986.
ISBN 0-297-78965-1

MCCART, Neil
Atlantic Liners of the Cunard Line: from 1884 to the Present Day by Neil McCart.
Patrick Stephens, Wellingborough, Northants., 1990.
ISBN 1-85260-065-9

MURRAY, Marischal
Union-Castle Chronicle, 1853-1953 by Marischal Murray.
Longmans, Green, London, 1953.

RABSON, Stephen
P and O: a Fleet History by Stephen Rabson and Kevin O'Donoghue.
World Ship Society, Kendal, Cumbria, 1988.
ISBN 0-905617-45-2

SHIPPING
GENERAL

JORDAN, Roger W.
The World's Merchant Fleets 1939: the Particulars and Wartime Fates of 6000 Ships by Roger W. Jordan.
Chatham Publishing, London, 1999.
ISBN 1-86176-023-X

Lloyd's Register of Shipping.
Lloyd's, London.
Annual publication.
(Printed Books holdings, from 1914-1940, are very incomplete).

The Mercantile Navy List and Maritime Directory.
HMSO, London.
Annual publication.
(Printed Books holdings, from 1914-1966, are very incomplete).

MILLER, William H.
Transatlantic Liners at War: the Story of the Queens by
William H. Miller and David F. Hutchings.
David and Charles, Newton Abbot, 1985.
ISBN 0-7153-8511-9

MITCHELL, W.H.
British Standard Ships of World War I by W.H. Mitchell and
L.A. Sawyer.
Sea Breezes, Liverpool, 1968.

MITCHELL, W.H.
*The Empire Ships: a Record of British-Built and Acquired
Merchant Ships During the Second World War* by W.H.
Mitchell and L.A. Sawyer.
2nd. ed.; Lloyds of London Press, London, 1990.
ISBN 1-85044-275-4

OSBORNE, Richard
Conversion for War edited by Dr. Richard Osborne.
World Ship Society, Kendal, 1983.
ISBN 0-905617-25-8 (pbk.)

PLUMMER, Russell
The Ships that Saved an Army: a Comprehensive Record of the 1300 'Little Ships' of Dunkirk by Russell Plummer.
Patrick Stephens, Wellingborough, Northants., 1990.
ISBN 1-85260-210-4

INDIVIDUAL

BROWNING, Marion
Uganda: the Story of a Very Special Ship written by Marion Browning ... [et al].
SS Uganda Trust, Broadstone, Dorset, 1998.
ISBN 0-9531082-0-1

Canberra: the Great White Whale.
Patrick Stephens, Cambridge, 1983.
ISBN 0-85059-636-X

HARDING, Steve
Gray Ghost: the R.M.S. Queen Mary at War by Steve Harding.
Pictorial Histories Publishing, Missoula, Montana, 1982.
ISBN 0-933126-26-3 (pbk.)

HICKEY, Des
Seven Days to Disaster: the Sinking of the Lusitania by Des Hickey and Gus Smith.
Collins, London, 1981.
ISBN 0-00-216882-0

KONINGS, Chris
Queen Elizabeth at War: His Majesty's Transport, 1939-1946 by Chris Konings.
Patrick Stephens, Wellingborough, Northants., 1985.
ISBN 0-85059-725-0

STEELE, James
Queen Mary by James Steele.
Phaidon Press, London, 1995.
ISBN 0-7148-2891-2

THOMAS, David A.
Queen Mary and the Cruiser: the Curacoa Disaster by David
A. Thomas and Patrick Holmes.
Leo Cooper, London, 1997.
ISBN 0-85052-548-9

WEST, John L.
The Loss of 'Lancastria' compiled by John L. West.
Millgate, Rossendale, Lancashire, 1988.
ISBN 1-870788-04-4

LIFE IN THE MERCHANT NAVY

BENNETT, G.H.
Survivors: British Merchant Seamen in the Second World War
by G.H. and R. Bennett.
Hambledon Press, London, 1999.
ISBN 1-85285-182-1

LANE, Tony
The Merchant Seamen's War by Tony Lane.
Manchester University Press, Manchester, 1990.
ISBN 0-7190-2397-1

Research Facilities at the Imperial War Museum

THE READING ROOM

The Department of Printed Books and the Department of Documents share a Reading Room in the Dome of the main building in Lambeth Road. The room is round, with a narrow gallery, and of considerable historical interest in itself as it used to be the chapel during the building's previous use as the Royal Bethlem Hospital, or Bedlam. A large plaque displaying the Ten Commandments dominates the room and we like to think that our readers respond nobly to its enjoinders, although the occasional, wistful and rather covetous glance at a neighbour's tempting array of books and documents has been observed!

The Reading Room is open to the public from Monday to Saturday between the hours of 10.00am and 5.00pm. It is closed on Sundays, Saturdays that fall on Bank Holiday weekends, Christmas Eve, Christmas Day, Boxing Day, and the last two full weeks of November for our annual stock-taking. Access is free but please let us know in advance that you are coming.

When making an appointment please give us as much detail of your area of research as possible. Material can then be pre-selected and be ready on your arrival. However, this should not deter you from a further catalogue search of your own. We will be happy to show you the various catalogues and options open to you. Bags are not generally allowed in the Reading Room - these should be left in the cloakroom - although handbags and portable computers are admissible. Please remember that this is an older building and, although we have done much to improve the provision of electric points, lighting and ventilation, we are limited by the amount of physical space actually available. We will, however, always try to accommodate anyone wishing to consult our collections. The design limitations of this old building make access to the Reading Room difficult for many disabled visitors but alternative facilities are available. Please ask when making your appointment.

Photocopying and other services
Guidance on photocopying procedures is available in printed form in the Reading Room itself. We are bound by the copyright law, and by our own conservation and preservation require-ments. Black and white photocopies are available at the fixed Museum price (at the time of writing) of 33 pence per sheet (no more than A3 size). Special photography can be arranged subject to a facility fee. Booklists are available on a variety of subjects.

Department of Printed Books Reprint Publications

We have a flourishing reprint programme. Copies of our catalogue are available free on request.

The family researcher is likely to find our official history reprints of particular interest, providing as they do, useful and detailed background to the campaigns fought. The British series of text volumes for the First World War is complete, and includes the full set of text volumes entitled *Naval Operations* by Corbett and Newbolt, and *Seaborne Trade* by Ernest Fayle. The former covers Royal Naval actions, while the latter concerns the Merchant Navy. Although we have not yet reprinted the map volumes for Corbett and Newbolt, we have reproduced a map volume for Fayle's history. As yet, only the last volume (volume III, part II) of the Second World War British official history, *War at Sea* by Roskill has been reprinted.

Other titles reprinted include an exact facsimile reproduction of two *Blighty Magazine* Christmas issues for 1916 and 1917 (a trench magazine free to troops at the Front, but subscribed to by the civilian population); Second World War Ministry of Information pamphlets on schools, the Fire Service in London, women in the factories, fashion and rationing; books by notable poets, writers and artists; War Office handbooks on the various armies of both world wars; occasional books based on works or collections held in the department - K. W. Mitchinson's *Gentlemen and Officers* on the London Rifle Brigade in the First World War, and David Williams' history of the 56th Division in the Second World War, *Black Cats at War*; and other internally produced guides or catalogues to some of our special collections. For full details and prices please see the catalogue, which is now available on our web-page, or contact the department. Telephone enquiries are welcome on: 020 7416 5346.

USEFUL CONTACTS

Department of Printed Books
Imperial War Museum
Lambeth Road, London SE1 6HZ
Tel: 020 7416 5342 (for general enquiries and appointments)
Fax: 020 7416 5246
E-mail: books@iwm.org.uk

For information and reservations relating to the **Department of Documents'** collection the address is the same as the above, with the following additions:

Tel: 020 7416 5221 / 5222 / 5223
Fax: 020 7416 5374
E-mail: docs@iwm.org.uk

Other collecting departments
The Museum's other collecting departments - the Photograph Archive, the Film and Video Archive, the Sound Archive, the Department of Exhibits and Firearms and the Department of Art - also have reading or visitors' rooms. Again, access is free but you must make an appointment. To make sure that the material you require is available, contact the Department concerned at least 24 hours in advance, and Departments such as the Film and Video Archive need 5-7 days notice to arrange viewing of particular film. Some departments also have elements of their collection stored off-site and such material may take longer to supply. A general guide to the research facilities, *The Collections: an Access Guide*, is available free upon request.

Again, disabled visitors are welcome, but are advised to notify the respective department of their needs in advance.

General Contacts:

The Museum has four branches. These are:

Imperial War Museum

Lambeth Road, London SE1 6HZ

Open daily, 10.00am-6.00pm

Tel: 020 7416 5000

Fax: 020 7416 5374

E-mail: mail@iwm.org.uk

Web site: www.iwm.org.uk

Recorded information: 020 7820 1683

Cabinet War Rooms

Clive Steps, Charles Street, London SW1A 2AQ

Open daily

Summer (1 April-30 September)

9.30am-6.00pm

last admission 5.15pm

Winter 10.00am-5.00pm, last admission 4.15pm

Tel: 020 7930 6961

Fax: 020 7839 5897

E-mail: cwr@iwm.org.uk

Duxford Airfield

Duxford, Cambridge CB2 4QR

Open daily

Summer (end March-mid October)

10.00am-6.00pm

Winter 10.00am-4.00pm

Tel: 01223 835000

Fax: 01223 837267

E-mail: duxford@iwm.org.uk

HMS *Belfast*

Morgan's Lane, Tooley Street, London SE1 2JH
Open daily
Summer (1 March-31 October)
10.00-6.00pm
Last admission 5.15pm
Winter 10.00am-5.00pm, last admission 4.15pm
Tel: 020 7407 6434
Fax: 020 7403 0719
E-mail: hmsbelfast@iwm.org.uk

All sites are closed 24, 25, 26 December

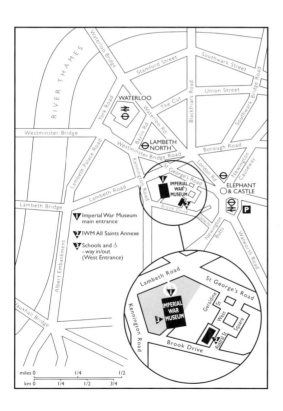